1

The First People came a long, long time ago.

3

There were big cold deserts.

5

The sea was much lower. There was more land. The Earth was colder.

7

The new land had many special animals. This is the kangaroo.

9

The water has crocodiles. The crocodile can hide in the water.

The river had fish to eat.

13

There were many birds to eat.

15

Some areas were very cold and icy.

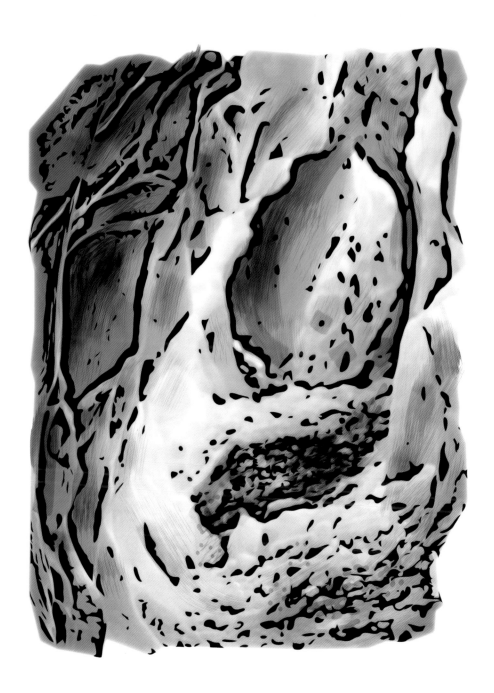

17

The First People moved down
into Australia.

19

The First People were in different tribes.

21

Possum fur made warm coats for cold places.

23

Word bank

first

people

time

deserts

lower

land

Earth

colder

special

animals

kangaroo

crocodile

river

birds

areas

Australia

different

tribes

possum

fur